CAMBRIDGE
UNIVERSITY PRESS

CAMBRIDGE
Global English Starters

Activity Book A

Kathryn Harper & Gabrielle Pritchard

SARIA

LAN

ANA

NASREEN

ARON

MANSI

3

1 Come into my class!

1 Think about it What can we do in class?

 1a Listen, say and circle.

"It's a ..." "It's a pencil."

1b Listen, check and repeat.

1

2

3

4

5

6

2 ⇅ Look and guess.
Join and check.

1 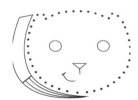 book

2  crayon

3  paper

4  pencil

🎧 **3b** **Listen, check and say.**

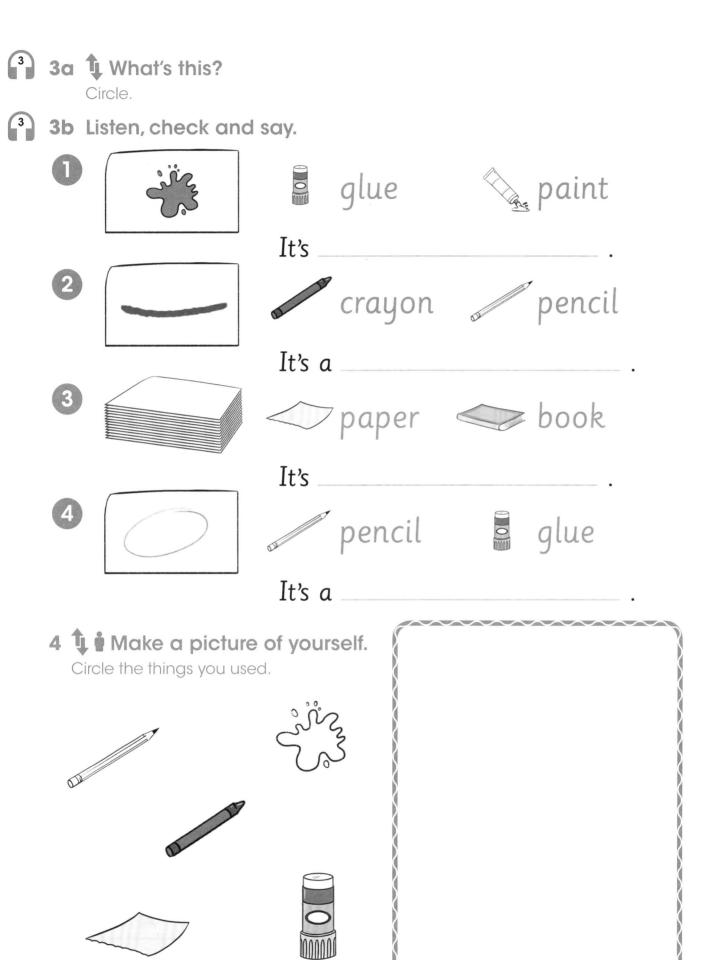

1

🖌 glue   🖌 paint

It's _____.

2

🖍 crayon   ✏ pencil

It's a _____.

3

📄 paper   📖 book

It's _____.

4

✏ pencil   🖌 glue

It's a _____.

4 ⇅ 👤 **Make a picture of yourself.**
  Circle the things you used.

2 Story time The Classroom

1 💭 Draw lines to show when things happen in the story.

2 💭 How do they feel?

Draw the faces for the beginning and end of the story.

3 💭 ⇅ **What is missing from this picture?**
Draw the things then trace the words.

☐ crayon ☐ paint ☐ pencil ☐ paintbrush

4 🧍 **Make your own special crayon.**
Show it to the class.

5 💭 **Values: Why is it important to tidy up?**
Show where to put the things.

3 Talk about it Old and new

🎧 4 **1** ↕ **Listen and circle or trace a or an.**
Then listen and repeat.

a *an*   *a* *an*

a *an*   *a* *an*

a *an*   *a* *an*

2a 👤 **Draw what's in your school bag.**

2b Ask and answer.

What's this?

It's …

3a Find 3 old things in this picture.
What are they?

3b Trace or write about 1 of the objects.

It's a ruler crayon pencil book pen pencil case.

It's a _____ .

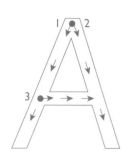  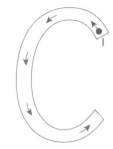

1 Say and match.

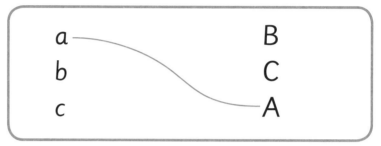

a   B

b   C

c   A

2 Listen and circle.

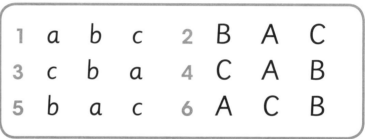

1	a	b	c		2	B	A	C
3	c	b	a		4	C	A	B
5	b	a	c		6	A	C	B

3 Listen and write.

Anna eats __n __pple.

The __ook and __rush are in the __lue __ag.

__at __atches a __rayon in a __ap.

4b Let's learn our numbers

1 Count and circle.
Then colour and say.

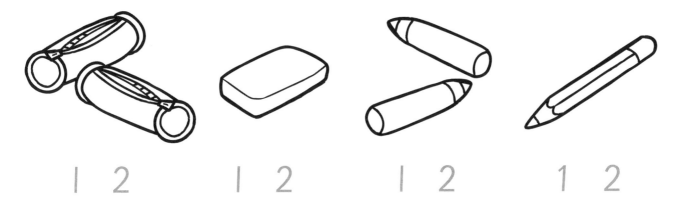

| 2 | 2 | 2   1 2

2 Find old and new things.
Count and write.

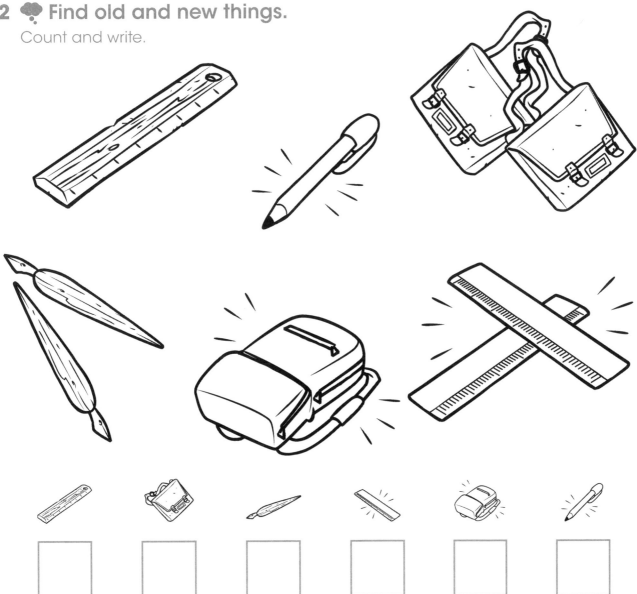

5 Find out more   The shapes of things

1 Colour, trace and say.

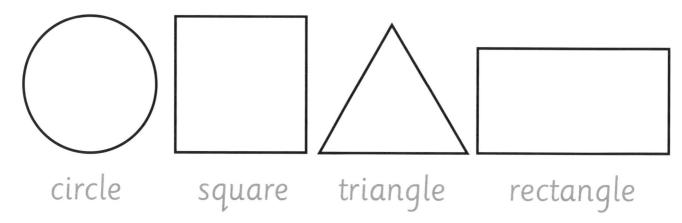

circle   square   triangle   rectangle

2a Colour and continue the patterns on the snakes.
Say.

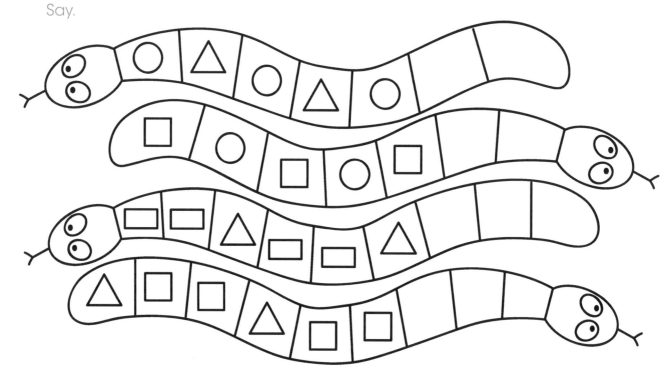

2b Make a new pattern.

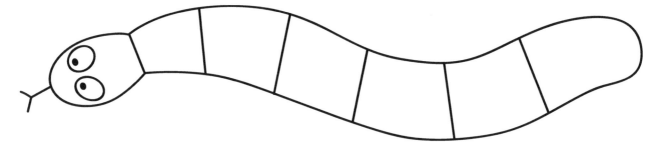

3a 💬 Look at the objects and trace the shapes you see.

3b ↕ Trace the correct word.

circle   square   triangle   rectangle

circle   square   triangle   rectangle

circle   square   triangle   rectangle

circle   square   triangle   rectangle

4 👤 ↕ Choose a shape and make a picture.

Use the shape as many times as you can. Show your picture to the class.

6 I can do it! Go on a scavenger hunt

1a Look, find and tick ✓.

 ☐   ☐   ☐   ☐

 ☐   ☐   ☐   ☐

1b What is missing? Draw.

2a Look, find and tick ✓.

B ☐   1 ☐   c ☐   A ☐

2 ☐   b ☐   a ☐   C ☐

2b What is missing? Write.

3a Look, find and tick ✓.

3b What is missing? Draw.

4a Look, find and tick ✓.

4b What is missing? Draw.

We are stars!

1 Think about it How are we different?

🎧 7 **1a** Listen, say and point.

🎧 8 **1b** Listen and tick ✓.

2a 💭 Complete the picture.

2b ⇕ Draw arrows and colour.

eyes

mouth

ears

nose

face

🎧 **3** ↕ Listen and colour.

1

The hair is yellow.

2

The eyes are green.

3

The nose is blue.

4

The mouth is red.

4 👤↕ **What's your favourite animal?**
Draw and colour.

Look at my _____ . The eyes are _____ .

2 Story time Elephant and Mouse

1a Which picture is from the start of the story?
Colour.

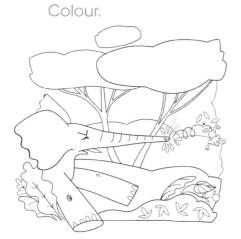  

1b Which picture is from the end of the story?
Colour.

2 💭 Look at the picture.
What's wrong? Circle.

3a Complete the picture.

3b Trace the words and draw lines to the parts of the faces.

face

eye

mouth

ear

nose

4 👤 **Make your own Elephant or Mouse puppet.**
Make up your own Elephant and Mouse story.

5 💬 **Values.**
Why is it good to be different?
How are they different? How do they help? Join and say.

3 **Talk about it** Funny families

 1a Look, listen and colour.

1b ⇅ Match the words to the aliens.
Trace and say.

1c Talk about the aliens.

dad   mum   sister   brother

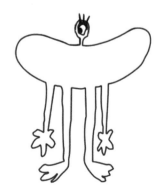

2a 🙋 Draw and colour an alien.

2b Pretend you're the alien.
Say some sentences about yourself.

3 ⬍ Trace the sentences and draw pictures or write words.

I'm an alien.

I've got _____ .

I've got _____ .

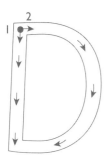

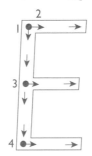

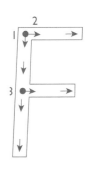

1 Say and match.

d	F
e	D
f	E

2 Listen and circle.

1	d	e	f		2	E	F	D
3	f	d	e		4	D	F	E
5	f	e	d		6	E	D	F

3 Listen, trace and write.

___ad ___ances with a ___uck.

___lephant has ___leven ___ggs.

___our ___at ___ish ___ly over a ___ence.

1 ⬍ Look, colour and count.

3   4   3   4

2 💭 Look at the monster family.
Find and write.

dad   mum   brothers   sisters

|

1 ⇅ Listen and make faces.

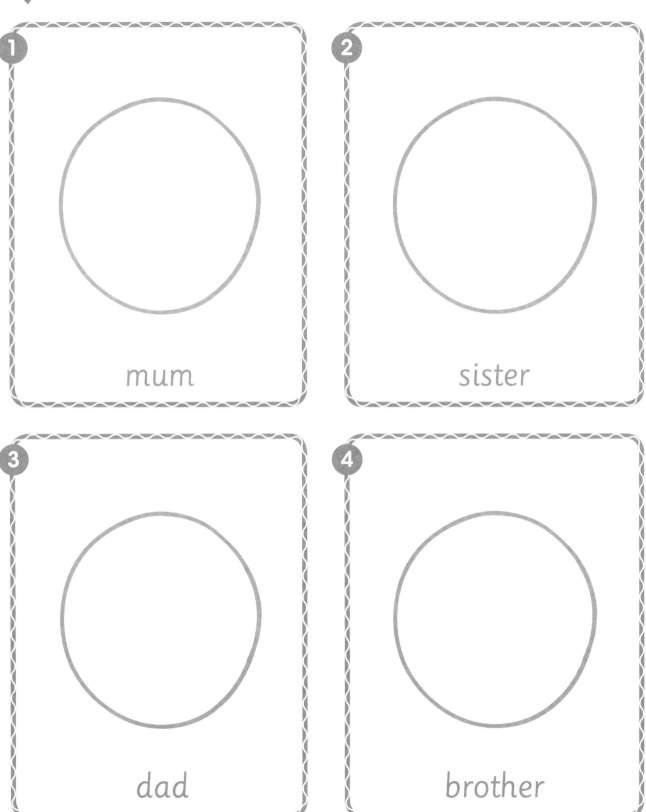

1   mum

2   sister

3   dad

4   brother

2 👤↕ **Show your pictures to the class.**
Talk about the faces.

3 💭 **How do the materials make the pictures different?**

4 👤💭 **Which is your favourite picture?**
Why?

_____ is my favourite.

6 I can do it! Go on a scavenger hunt

1a Look, find and tick ✓.

 ☐   ☐   ☐

☐   ☐   ☐

1b What is missing? Draw.

2a Look, find and tick ✓.

F ☐   3 ☐   D ☐   E ☐

d ☐   4 ☐   e ☐   f ☐

2b What is missing? Write.

3a Look, find and tick ✓.

[ ] [ ] [ ] [ ]

3b What is missing? Draw.

4a Look, find and tick ✓.

[ ] [ ] [ ]

[ ] [ ] [ ]

4b What is missing? Draw.

We are stars!

3 Feelings

1 Think about it   What makes you happy or sad?

🎧 14   **1** Listen and match.

1 **2** **3** **4** **5** **6**

2 💭 ⇅ Match to what they need.

I'm hungry.   I'm cold.   I'm thirsty.   I'm hot.

3 Listen, find and colour the faces.

happy

sad

hungry

thirsty

4 Write your name.
Draw and colour your face.

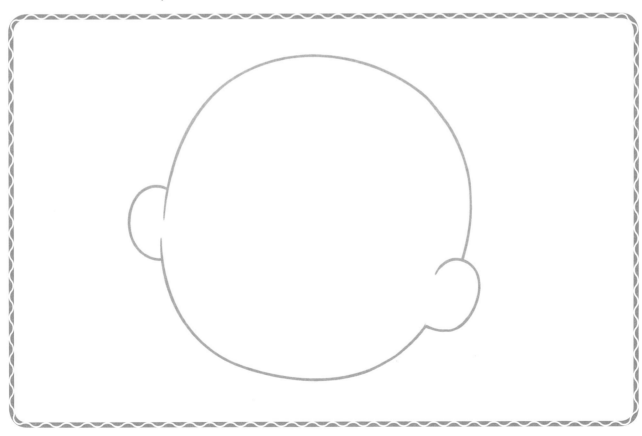

I'm _____ . I'm happy ☺ .

29

1 ⇅ 👤 Colour your favourite character.

 Daddy Bear

 Baby Bear

 Mummy Bear

 Goldilocks

2 ⇅ 💭 How do these things make them feel?
Match and trace the words.

            scared

            sad

            angry

            hungry

3 **How do these things make <u>you</u> feel?**

Match and trace the words.

 scared

 sad

 angry

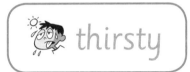 hungry

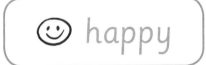 happy

thirsty

4 **Values.**

Why is it good to be kind?

Goldilocks is scared. Baby Bear is kind to her.

Look at the pictures. Are the children kind?
Colour the heart ♡ where the children are kind.

Choose 1 picture and act out how you can be kind.

1 Match to he or she.
Then say.

He is hot.

she   he

🎧 16 **2** ↕ **Listen and trace the correct speech bubble.**

I'm thirsty.

We're thirsty.

We're happy.

I'm happy.

I'm angry.

We're angry.

I'm scared.

We're scared.

3 👤 **Draw yourself and show your friends.**

Then tick ✓, trace or write the words.

How do you feel?

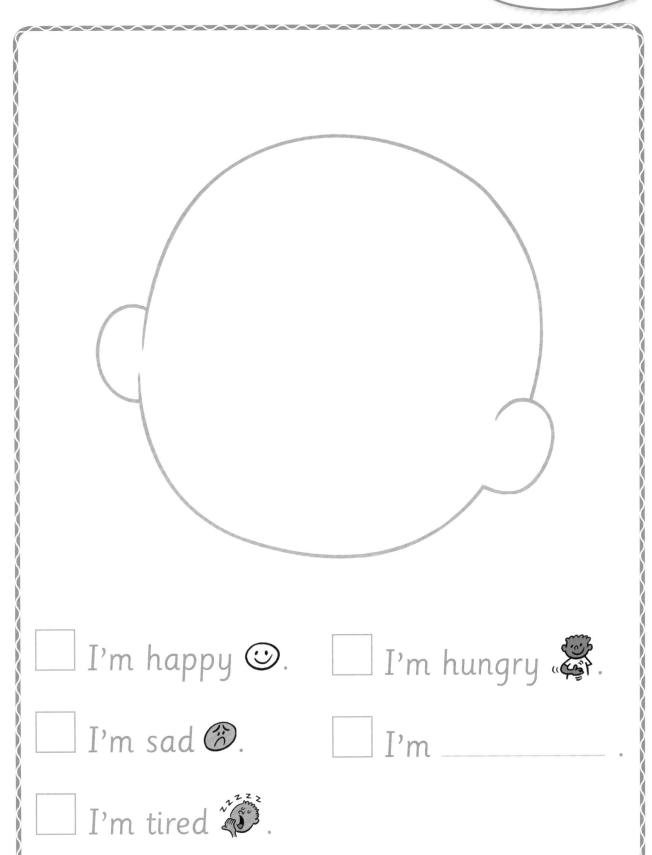

☐ I'm happy ☺.   ☐ I'm hungry 🧒.

☐ I'm sad 😣.   ☐ I'm _____ .

☐ I'm tired 😴.

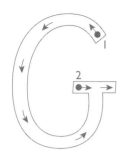 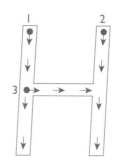 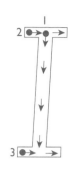

1 Say and match.

g		H
h		I
i		G

2 Listen and circle.

1	g h i	2	H G I
3	i h g	4	I G H
5	h g i	6	G I H

3 Listen, trace and write.

___oldilocks ___ets a ___uitar.

___anna ___as a sore ___and.

___mogen opens the ___nsect jar.

1 ⇕ Count and match.
Then colour and say.

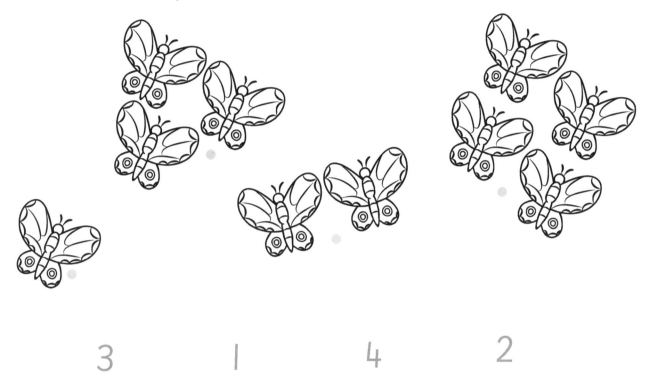

3   1   4   2

2 💭 ⇕ What starts with these letters?
Find, count and write how many words start with **g**, **h** or **i**.

g   h   i

5 Find out more Hot and cold

1a Colour the pictures for hot 🔥 and cold ❄️.

1b ↕️ Match to **hot** or **cold**.

1c 💭 Count the hot and cold things.
Trace or write the number.

hot 🔥 ⟶ 1 2 3 4 ___

cold ❄️ ⟶ 1 2 3 4 ___

2 🧍 It's a hot and sunny day.

Draw what you like to eat.

Is it hot or cold?

3 🧍 It's a cold and rainy day.

Draw what you like to eat.

Is it hot or cold?

6 I can do it! Go on a scavenger hunt

1a Look, find and tick ✓.

1b What is missing? Draw.

2a Look, find and tick ✓.

4 ☐   H ☐   3 ☐   i ☐   G ☐

1 ☐   h ☐   I ☐   2 ☐   g ☐

2b What is missing? Write.

☐

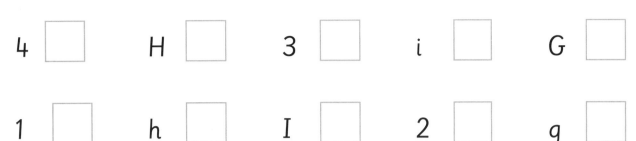

3 Listen and colour.
Then search, find and write the number.

1  _____

2 _____

3 _____

4 _____

4 Look and find.
Count and write.

 _____

 _____

We are stars!

39